Somebody Out There Needs You!

by

DAVE WILLIAMS

Somebody Out There Needs You!

Somebody Out There Needs You

Second Printing *(Revised)* 2000

ISBN   0-938020-42-0

Published by

D E C A P O L I S
P U B L I S H I N G

Printed in the United States of America

MHC   10 9 8 7 6 5 4 3 2

OTHER BOOKS BY DAVE WILLIAMS

Contents

"The most lonely place in the world is the human heart when God is absent."

— *Unknown*

Chapter 1

Somebody Needs YOU!

At this very moment, as you read this book, there is somebody you know who is on the road to eternal damnation. Somebody needs *you* to show them the way to salvation! That somebody may be a friend, a coworker, a relative, or even an enemy; but that somebody needs you.

Religion Can Send People To Hell

Weekly, there are millions of people who go to church and worship a "God" they don't even know. They participate in the form of religion, but if they do not have a salvation relationship with Jesus Christ, it is an empty, meaningless exercise. They don't have a personal relationship with Jesus. They have never accepted Him as

Savior and been born again into God's Kingdom. Jesus said:

> Except a man be born again, he cannot see the kingdom of God.
>
> — John 3:3

Religion, without true salvation through Jesus Christ, will lead us to hell just as inevitably as a life of unrepentant sin. After death, those who practiced religion without a saving faith in Jesus Christ will find their spirits thrust into a dreadful place of torment and incarceration, to await their judgment at God's Great White Throne.

> And I saw a great white throne, and him that sat on it, from whose face the earth and the heaven fled away; and there was found no place for them. And I saw the dead, small and great, stand before God; and the books were opened: and another book was opened, which is the book of life: and the dead were judged out of those things which were written in the books, according to their works.
>
> And the sea gave up the dead which were in it; and death and hell delivered up the dead which were in them: and they were judged every man according to their works. And death and hell were cast into the lake of fire. This is the second death. And whosoever was not found written in the book of life was cast into the lake of fire.
>
> — Revelation 20:11-15

Hell Is Forever

Hell is real. It is a place of eternal regret; a place of hopelessness where mankind is forever separated from God! Every day, people are sucked down into hell through death's door. Religious and nonreligious people alike find the same eternal destiny. Why? Because religion cannot save us. Only Jesus Christ can save us.

Jesus said, "Ye must be born again." He didn't say, "Ye must be religious to see the Kingdom of God," but, "Ye must be born again." He was speaking of a spiritual birth that comes through simple, but genuine, personal faith in Jesus Christ as Savior. We are either saved through confession of our sins and faith in Jesus Christ as the Son of God — or we are lost, never having accepted Jesus' work on the cross for our salvation. Jesus said:

> **I am the way, the truth and the life: no man cometh unto the Father, but by me.**
>
> **— John 14:6**

The "Midnight Hour" Is Approaching

I had a vision ten years ago during an intercessory prayer meeting. As we worshiped, suddenly, through my "spiritual" eyes, I saw fog and clouds swirling densely around me. Emerging from the fog like a lighthouse beacon, I saw a grandfather clock. Immediately I noticed two distinct things about this clock. First, the time was 11:59 PM, one minute before midnight. Second, the clock's pendulum was drawn back ready to make its final swing which would bring the minute hand up to the midnight hour. I knew intuitively that when the clock reached midnight that the bridegroom would come for His Church. Jesus was showing me that time is running out. The end is closer than we think.

Recently, as I was praying, that same grandfather clock returned to me in another vision. It was still 11:59 PM, but as I watched, I saw something different this time. The pendulum was no longer ready to make its final swing. This time it had dropped and now hung straight down, halfway through its final swing. Time is desperately short. We are coming down to the last few moments of history.

Some time ago, Dr. Jack Van Impe, a Bible prophecy scholar, called me to chat about some important prophetic issues. He said, "There's an article here in the *Jerusalem Post* that says they have conclusive evidence that the battle of Gog, Magog, Meshech, and Tubal is imminent. They have found evidence that Russia and the Arab nations are planning a coalition invasion of the nation of Israel." This battle is prophesied in Ezekiel 38 and 39.

Many Bible scholars believe that the time Russia and the Arab nations invade Israel will be about the time Jesus will come for His Church and catch us off the earth. The dead in Christ will rise, and we which are alive will be caught up together to meet the Lord in the air, and so shall we ever be with the Lord (1 Thessalonians 4:16-17). It is interesting that the article said the war prophesied thousands of years ago is imminent.

Somebody out there needs you! Somebody, whether they practice a form of religion or are not religious at all, needs you to share Christ's plan of salvation. His plan is for everyone to go to heaven — the only alternative is hell. Wow! What awesome alternatives!

You Can Change Somebody's Destiny

You have abiding within you right now the power to affect a change in somebody's destiny.

The Holy Spirit has empowered you to be a soul winner. Jesus said:

> **But Ye shall receive power, after that the Holy Ghost is come upon you: and Ye shall be witnesses unto me both in Jerusalem, and in all Judea, and in Samaria, and unto the uttermost part of the earth.**
>
> **— Acts 1:8**

"But I'm no evangelist," you say. That may be true. Your gift may not be that of an evangelist, but that does not exclude you from being a soul winner. One of the greatest evangelists of all times, Charles Finney, was a lawyer. D. L. Moody, one of the greatest evangelists the world has ever seen from the Midwest, wasn't even an ordained minister. Smith Wigglesworth, a twentieth century apostle of faith, was a plumber. And Billy Sunday was a professional baseball player. These men were ordinary, simple people — just like you and me.

All you have to do is tell people what you have seen and heard. Just tell them what you know, and let the Holy Spirit do the rest.

A woman, who was blind, came to Mount Hope Church one day because her friend said, "I've heard that 'the church with the flags' believes in

healing. Let's go there and see if God will heal you."
Guess what? Because her friend acted on what he
had heard, that woman received her sight from
God. This report can be verified.

I was on the Internet one day, talking to some
people in England. One woman was very de-
pressed. I asked if I could pray for her, and I discovered she did not know Jesus as Savior, but
wanted to. So, I led her in a prayer for salvation.
Thank God for computers!

Spreading the Gospel is a great privilege that
does not, and should not, need to be burdensome;
it is the mistakes we make when trying to witness
that discourage us and make soul winning seem
like a hard task.

I am going to share with you twelve common
mistakes people make in soul winning. Learning
how to avoid these mistakes will help you evan-
gelize your friends, neighbors, and loved ones. You
can be an effective soul winner.

> **The fruit of the righteous is a tree of life; and he**
> **that winneth souls is wise.**
>
> **— Proverbs 11:30**

"If doing a good act in public will excite others to do more good, then . . . 'Let your Light shine to all . . ..' Miss no opportunity to do good."*

John Wesley

Chapter 2

Mistake One: Thinking The Whole Job Of Evangelism Is Up To The Minister And Those Who Are Gifted

Many Christians have adopted this attitude toward evangelism. "I don't have to witness," they say, "after all, that's why we have a minister, right?"

Wrong! That is not the way the Bible says we should think. God never calls pastors, apostles, prophets, evangelists, and teachers to be soul winners merely by virtue of their titles. As individuals, yes, they are to be soul winners, but the real reason God calls Christians into these five positions is to equip other believers for ministry. God wants *you* to be able to minister. It is the job of the "five-fold ministry" to build up the Body of Christ — the Church (Ephesians 4:11-12). God never intended for the majority of the Church to sit back and relax while only a select few do the work of the ministry.

Chapter 3

Mistake Two: Waiting Until All The Problems In Your Own Life Have Been Worked Out

How many times have you told yourself, "I'm just not good enough to witness for Christ. There are still some problems in my own life." If you have ever felt that way, I have news for you. As long as you are on the earth, there will be some kind of problem affecting your life.

People have problems; that's a fact. I'm not saying we can't overcome our problems as we place our trust in Jesus Christ, but throughout history we have seen how God can take an imperfect man, fill him with the Holy Spirit, and use him to shake and shape the world for Him. Some of the greatest soul winners were not trained ministers. Some of them had problems, but they still managed to lead thousands of people to Jesus Christ.

> The righteous cry, and the Lord heareth, and delivereth them out of ALL THEIR TROUBLES. The Lord is nigh unto them that are of a broken heart; and saveth such as be of a contrite spirit. Many are the afflictions of the righteous: BUT the Lord delivereth him OUT OF THEM ALL.
>
> — Psalm 34:17-19

You can share your faith now. Solved problems are not a prerequisite for effective evangelism. It wouldn't matter to me if an imperfect person led me to Christ. I would still be on my way to heaven. If nobody led me to Christ, just because they didn't feel "perfect enough," I would be doomed.

Don't let your earthly problems turn into someone's eternal disaster. Somebody out there needs an imperfect person, like you, to tell them about Jesus Christ. God is calling *you* to shake and shape the world for Christ.

Chapter 4

Mistake Three: Thinking That A Moral Life And "Letting Your Light Shine" Is Enough Of A Witness

It is true that Jesus said, "Ye are the light of the world," but He also said, "Go Ye into all the world and preach the Gospel." That means to go and proclaim the Word of God with your mouth as well as living a life-style of holiness. Simply letting your light shine is not good enough. Shining, alone, does not reveal the source of the light.

When you see a light bulb shining, its brightness does not explain why it glows. Before you can understand why a light bulb glows, you must first grasp the basic concepts of electricity, the combination of elements that make a light bulb, and the effect electricity has on those elements. The same is true for those who are unaware of your source of power. They may be drawn to you because of your brightness, but that doesn't mean they will understand what it is that makes you shine. If you don't reveal to them the "electricity" that makes your light shine, they will not recognize it is Jesus Christ.

The Bible tells us we can't expect people to know the truth unless we tell them. Faith comes by hearing (Romans 10:17). Somebody out there needs to *hear* from *you*! Just letting your light shine will not communicate the entire message. They need you to *tell* them the good news of Jesus Christ.

Chapter 5

Mistake Four: Not Believing God Will Back Us Up By Doing What He Has Promised To Do

The early Christians had a solid conviction. They believed the Gospel worked. In fact, they said, "There is no other name under heaven given among men whereby we must be saved." Have you ever looked up what the word "saved" actually means? The meaning is three-fold: It means *rescued*. It means *delivered*. It means *healed*. There is no other name whereby we can be rescued, delivered, and healed. Early Christians believed in the power of the Gospel. Believing the Gospel was not just an intellectual exercise, but a concrete, usable tool for evangelism. They spoke the Gospel believing it would work — and it did!

When Jesus said, "Go Ye into all the world," He also told about the signs that would follow the believer.

> And these signs shall follow them that believe; In my name shall they cast out devils; they shall speak with new tongues; They shall take up serpents; and if they drink any deadly thing, it shall not hurt them; they shall lay hands on the sick, and they shall recover.
>
> — Mark 16:17-18

Jesus didn't just command His followers to preach. Before He sent people out, He gave them the power to demonstrate the Gospel. The early Christians took that power and used it. As a result, many were healed, delivered, and, most importantly of all, many were saved. He is still giving that same power to His followers today.

Eutychus was raised from the dead. Witnesses of this miracle became believers. Paul was bitten by a poisonous snake. He shook it into the fire, was unharmed, and people witnessing this miracle believed. Sick people in Jerusalem lined the streets so that Peter's shadow might fall on them, and when it did, they were healed. What was the result of all these signs? The book of Acts states over and over again, ". . . and many were added to the church."

Today, things have changed. I don't mean to say God will not back us up like He did Peter, Philip, Paul, and others. I know He will. However, today, doubt has taken root in many believers' minds. Christians who do not understand clearly God's will on this subject are unsure how His promises apply to them. "If *I* lay hands on the sick," they wonder, "will they recover?" Uncertainty about what the modern Christian can do in Jesus' name has kept many believers from using the power God has given them, and that is not good.

It is the Gospel that holds the power to change lives.

Those who minister in Teen Challenge know that statement is true. They are so convinced God will back them with His power that they lay hands on the alcoholic, the drug addict, the person who is floundering in a mire of sin, and they believe He will deliver them. They *know* God will lift up the vilest sinner and set him on the solid foundation of Jesus Christ. They accept *as fact* that God can make a somebody out of a nobody. That is why Teen Challenge has been so successful.

You can be successful too. If you believe in Jesus Christ, when you witness to others, signs and miracles will follow you.

I have experienced this in my own life. Sick people have recovered when I told them about the healing power of Jesus Christ, laid hands on them, and prayed for them to be healed.

Signs, just like Jesus promised, have taken place in our church. A deaf girl's ears were opened during an altar call one Sunday morning.

Bound, oppressed, lost, and sick people arrive at the Mount Hope Care Clinic every Saturday morning, and many of them leave in an altogether different condition. When care workers who believe in the power of the Gospel lay hands on them and pray, sickness subsides, oppression flees, those who are bound experience new freedom in Jesus Christ, and what is the result? Unsaved people see the power of God in action, believe in Jesus Christ, and walk out of the Care Clinic saved and Spirit-filled.

The signs that Jesus talked about really do follow those who believe. I even know of a case where someone drank a poisonous substance and was not harmed. Early one morning, Shannon, a little girl who goes to our church, found some ant poison and drank it. When her parents woke up, they discovered what she had done. Can you imagine the thoughts that must have gone through their minds when they read the words, "Fatal if swallowed"? I'm sure pictures of a sick and dying little girl must have flashed into their minds. But, in the midst of their panic came these words, ". . . and if they drink any deadly thing, it shall not harm them." These parents are people who follow Jesus. They believe His Word is true so they prayed, "In Jesus' name, don't let any harm come to our daughter," and none did.

Whether someone needs healing, deliverance, or victory over Satan's lies in their life, in Jesus' name you can help them. Somebody out there needs *you*. When you believe that God will back you up with His power, then you will be able to change the world around you.

*"Preach the Gospel
every day; if necessary,
use words."*

— *St. Francis of Assisi*

Chapter 6

Mistake Five: Fear Of Not Knowing What To Say Or How To Say It

Have you ever found yourself in a jam because you knew the Holy Spirit wanted you to witness to someone, but you didn't know what to say?

I know what that is like. I remember a time when I was going to visit a relative of mine. I knew the Holy Spirit was prompting me to share the Gospel with her, and I stewed . . . I fretted . . . I struggled. I tried to figure out the right way for me to initiate a conversation about Jesus Christ, but all my rehearsing got me nowhere. When I saw her, I was thrilled because the Holy Spirit made it easy for me to witness. She was the one who steered the subject to Jesus. She asked me the questions.

All I had to do was open my mouth and tell her what I knew. The Holy Spirit could not have made it any easier for me to share my faith. He had already prepared her to receive the things I wanted to tell her.

There is no reason for you to fret or worry about what you are going to say. If you have prayed, the Holy Spirit has already gone ahead of you. He has paved the way for you to witness so you will not need to use high pressure tactics. You will not need to be a master of theology either.

When Philip witnessed to the Ethiopian eunuch, the Holy Spirit paved the way. Philip did not have to do anything to make the eunuch listen. The Ethiopian had already been reading the Scriptures. All he needed was for someone to come along and explain what Jesus offered. As soon as Philip did, the eunuch believed, was baptized, and went away rejoicing (Acts 8:26-39).

Naaman's little maid did not know much. But when she told Naaman what she did know, he acted on the truth and was healed (2 Kings 5:1-14). Sometimes God wants you to share a word of truth or a short testimony, and that is all. That may be all someone needs to hear at that particular moment. You should not feel pressured to do or say more.

Somebody out there needs *you* to tell them what you have seen, what you have heard, and what you have experienced. They are waiting for you to tell them what you know.

"There was nothing to reconcile. Our relationship was never broken."

— Billy Graham
(about his son, Franklin)

Chapter 7

Mistake Six: Nagging, Pushing, And Being Argumentative

Can you think of an example where Jesus nagged, pushed, or argued someone into the Kingdom of Heaven? No. Jesus didn't do that, neither should you.

So many people make the mistake of trying to push their loved ones to Christ. "Hey, you old sinner," they say in a smug tone of voice, "when are you going to get saved?" Then they add insult to injury by saying things like, "I'm the only spiritual one around here." Or, they may not say any words at all but their attitude shows it. When we try to coerce an unbeliever, we are showing our lack of trust in the Holy Spirit. We feel we have got to *do* something to save this person — so we nag. But, instead of nagging, pushing, and arguing, we should be demonstrating the love and commitment of Jesus Christ. Then be ready with the answer when that person asks, "What makes you so different?" Once he asks, the door is open for you to share Jesus with him. You can share why you are filled with hope and how he can be filled with hope too (1 Peter 3:15).

When Billy Graham's son strayed from the Lord, because he did not nag his son about his lapse of faith, it did not affect the relationship they had with each other. They still hugged. They still played ball together. They still told each other, "I love you." When his son came back to Jesus, the media asked Billy, "What was your emotional response when you reconciled with your son?" "I never had anything against him," Billy replied, "and he never had anything against me. There was nothing to reconcile. Our relationship was never broken."

This "earthly" relationship reflects our relationship to our Heavenly Father. Even when we turn away from Him and His gift of salvation, He still loves us. When we accept Him and "come home" He is waiting for us with open arms.

Keith Miller, the writer of *A Taste of New Wine*, had a little different experience. When he became Spirit-filled, he began to nag his wife. "Come on," he would tell her. "You need this, too." The more he nagged her, the more she turned away. Finally, one day while Keith was praying, the Lord said to him, "Why don't you start being more committed to that woman than you've ever been before? Take the garbage out. Help her more. Show her the change that has taken place in your life." Keith listened to the Lord and took His advice. In just a couple of weeks his wife was filled with the Holy Spirit. Now she and Keith share the same wonderful relationship with God.

Nagging, pushing, and arguing will only put people on the defensive. These things can only produce the opposite of the intended effect. People will be driven farther away from God. Somebody out there needs *you* to love them. Somebody out there needs your commitment. It may be a family member. It may be a friend or a neighbor, but somebody out there needs your love.

"We want to be contagious Christians, don't we? Then let's be real with people."

— *Bill Hybels*

Chapter 8

Mistake Seven: Being "Over Spiritual" To The Point Of Making People Feel Uncomfortable

Years ago I clipped a letter out of the newspaper. It was written to Ann Landers by a mother who was fed up with her super-spiritual son. No matter what the occasion, he had a Scripture quotation ready. If the UPS man came to the door, he would say something about Jesus coming soon and then quote, "Behold I stand at the door and knock…." The mother couldn't take it anymore.

You know, Jesus did quote Scripture, but He quoted it to the devil — for a reason! This woman's son just expounded on the Scriptures whenever he felt like it. Maybe his intentions were good, but they alienated his mother from the Gospel. As far as the mother was concerned, he had developed an "I'm better than you" attitude.

Sometimes that happens when people have just been baptized in the Holy Spirit. Spirit-filled people are no better than non-Spirit-filled people. They have that second work of grace, but that should not give them any reason to act superior. A superior attitude will only drive people away, and that is completely opposite of the goal you want to achieve. If anything, Spirit-filled people should be even better equipped to attract others to Christ. People should be looking at you and saying to themselves, "I want what that person has." Don't let a super-spiritual superior attitude drive the lost away.

Another mistake that falls in this category is becoming too involved. Filled with the desire to exercise newly found Holy Spirit anointings, newly Spirit-filled believers run the risk of overdoing it. Every time the church opens its doors they are there. By doing so, they may create the illusion that unless someone is constantly at church they are not spiritual. Believers must be involved, but not beyond common sense. One person cannot do everything and should not try. Family responsibilities will end up being neglected which will lead to resentment by other family members. The goal is to bring your family together *in* Christ, not alienate your spouse or children because there is no time for them.

Somebody out there needs *you* to show them a true picture of Jesus Christ. Jesus did not act superior, but He always demonstrated love and compassion to those around Him. Love and compassion will go much further in winning lost souls to Him than super-spiritual zealousness.

"When Christians begin to pray for the felt needs of the lost, God surprises them with almost immediate answers."

— *Ed Silvoso*

Chapter 9

Mistake Eight: Failing To Pray

A little lady went to the preacher one day and asked, "Why is my son not saved?"

"Because your eyes aren't wet enough," was the preacher's response.

Psalm 126:5 says this: "They that sow in tears shall reap in joy." Prayer is the single most important factor in soul winning. Unsaved people are spiritually blind, but through prayer, they are loosed from their blindness. And once they are set free, the light of the Gospel will be able to shine into their inner spiritual darkness, and they will be able to see the truth.

> For the weapons of our warfare are not carnal, but mighty through God to the pulling down of strongholds.
>
> — 2 Corinthians 10:4

Don't make the mistake of getting mad at your unsaved friends and loved ones when they do things, or want you to do things, that are contrary to your Christian beliefs. You would not get mad at a blind man if he ran into you, would you? By the same token, you should not get angry with people who are spiritually blind. They may "bump into" your faith at times, but don't condemn them, pray for them. Pray that the Holy Spirit will open their eyes and send the right people to cross their paths with the true message of Jesus Christ.

One preacher challenged his congregation to write down the names of the people they wanted to see saved. Then they prayed for these people every day. Eighty-three names on prayer requests were turned in during that service. Within four weeks, sixty-two of those eighty-three people were saved. Prayer does work. Somebody out there needs _your_ prayers.

Chapter 10

Mistake Nine: Failing To Keep The Conversation Simple

Christians often come on too strong, too fast, with too much. We try to give the whole message in an avalanche of words, when just a simple word of truth is all the Holy Spirit wants us to share.

There are many "gimmicky" approaches that can turn people from the Lord.

If someone asks you, "Hey buddy, got a match?" Don't come back with an answer like this: "Well, I haven't had a match since the great explosion that took place when I became a Christian." The chances are good that you will not impress anybody with a line like that. In fact, the odds are tremendous that you will just look silly.

Prefabricated "lines" cannot meet the demands of different situations. Try to avoid them. Just be sensitive to the needs of people, and follow the leading of the Holy Spirit. That way you will be able to say the right words at the appropriate time and be truly helpful. As a result, you will not look foolish, and the person you are talking to will not suffer the pain of embarrassment.

The message of the Gospel is simple. Somebody out there needs to hear a few simple words from *you*.

Chapter 11

Mistake Ten: Sowing Mingled Seed

We harvest what we plant. That is a fact. What is more, it is one of God's laws.

> **Be not deceived; God is not mocked: for what-soever a man soweth, that shall he also reap.**
>
> **— Galatians 6:7**

There are some people who mock God by saying, "That's nonsense; you don't reap what you sow." But they are wrong. If you plant corn, you do not harvest peanuts, do you? No. You *do* reap what you sow. And if you sow mingled seed, you *will* get a messed up harvest. What do I mean by mingled seed?

When you claim salvation for your family, don't mess up the harvest by making comments like, "The way you act, you're never going to get saved." That is sowing mingled seed. It is like contaminating blue grass seed with dandelion seed — mixing good seed with bad.

The Bible says in Mark 11:24, "What things soever ye desire, when ye pray, believe that ye receive them, and ye shall have them." Do you desire to see your family saved? Do you desire to see your friend or neighbor saved? If you do, then when you pray, believe that your prayers have been answered. Sow the promises of God's Word, and don't back down.

I once worked with a man who struggled against terrible circumstances. He was a mess, and it finally cost him his job. Occasionally, however, the opportunity would arise for me to share a little word of truth from the Gospel with him, so I did — without any noticeable results. Finally, the day came when this man was leaving for good. As he walked out for the last time, I looked him straight in the eye and said, "Man, God loves you, and He is going to get a hold of you."

Now, I could have told him he was no good. I could have informed him that his destination was the gutter, and ultimately, he would blister in hell for the rest of eternity. But that would have been mixed seed. I was praying for Billy and believed God would save him. I put my mouth where my faith was.

> **We having the same spirit of faith, according as it is written, I believed, and therefore have I spoken; we also believe, and therefore speak.**
>
> **— 2 Corinthians 4:13**

One day I was sitting in my car listening to a tape, when a man walked up to me. There was a radiance about this guy. He had a twinkle in his eye and a happy smile on his face. When he told me who he was, I was amazed at the change in his life. The same man who used to be drunk or high on drugs all the time was a completely different person. God *did* get a hold of him! Now he is saved; his life is straightened out, and he is winning others for Christ.

> **Therefore if any man be in Christ, he is a new creature: old things are passed away; behold, all things are become new.**
>
> **— 2 Corinthians 5:17**

When you sow seed, make it good seed. Pray, then believe the Holy Spirit will do His work on that seed. When you do, your seed will spring up into a beautiful harvest. Somebody out there needs *you*. Plant some seeds of faith on their behalf, and get ready to reap the harvest.

Chapter 12

Mistake Eleven: Not Visualizing Properly

There is no doubt in my mind that there are people in the world today who are teaching visualization techniques that are contrary to what the Bible teaches. They want you to "use the power of your mind" to bring into reality whatever you visualize. They teach you to place your faith in your own thoughts rather than in Jesus Christ — and that is not what I mean by visualization.

The acceptable form of visualization bridges the gap between the soul and the spirit. Jesus gave us an example of this when He said in John 4:35, "Lift up your eyes and look on the fields; for they are white already to harvest." In that passage Jesus was telling the disciples to visualize the great number of souls that were ready to be harvested.

Can you visualize that harvest? Lift up your eyes and look on the fields. Do you see a harvest that is ripe and ready to be picked, a harvest made not of grain, but of human souls? A harvest made up of people you know?

Go ahead; picture them in church with their hands lifted up. See them not as they are but as you desire them to be — saved! Pray for them. Picture Jesus having a special encounter with them. See it in the eye of your imagination, the eye that bridges the gap between the soul and the spirit.

Somebody out there needs *you* to see them in a new light. Look at them through the eyes of your imagination, and see them as they could be in Christ. Then, ask the Father to give you the desires of your heart, in Jesus' name.

Chapter 13

Mistake Twelve: Failing To Follow Through

Christianity without community is like an ocean without water. Once you lead someone to Christ and His Church, their involvement in small groups where they can be discipled adequately is imperative. You cannot simply befriend a person until they are saved and then move on to someone else.

To the new convert, the fellowship, strength, and support of other, more mature brothers and sisters in the Lord is the catalyst they need in order to grow.

As in physical growth, where a child becomes an adult, so must "baby" Christians grow to spiritual adulthood. Part of your job is to help them grow. You must help them along until they are ready to stand on their own. That is what Jesus did for His disciples. He trained and equipped them until they were ready to take over after He left.

Somebody out there needs *you* to help him get "plugged in" and make sure he receives the spiritual sustenance he needs to grow in faith.

Chapter 14

Conclusion

Remember: You have what the world is looking for!

Somebody out there needs you — just the way you are — to tell them how they can find new life through Jesus Christ.

Somebody out there needs to not only see your light shine but also to hear about Jesus Christ, the source behind your light.

Somebody is waiting for you to step out in faith, so God can back you up with the right words to say and the supernatural power you will need in order to demonstrate the Gospel.

Somebody needs to be seen through the eyes of your imagination, as he could be in Christ. He needs you to sow seeds of faith into his life.

Somebody needs to feel your love, your patience, your friendship, and the power behind your prayers as you gently lead them to the Savior.

Somebody out there needs you, first to tell him how he can be saved and then to help him grow to maturity in the Lord.

You could be the one to kindle growth in some newly born-again person. If you are willing to let the Holy Spirit use you and work through you, then God will equip you with everything you need to be a successful soul winner!

Somebody out there needs YOU!

About The Author

Dave Williams is pastor of Mount Hope Church and International Outreach Ministries, with world headquarters in Lansing, Michigan. He has served for 20 years, leading the church in Lansing from 226 to over 4,000 today. Dave sends trained ministers into unreached cities to establish disciple-making churches, and, as a result, today has "branch" churches in the United States, Philippine Islands, and Africa.

Dave is the founder and president of Mount Hope Bible Training Institute, a fully accredited institute for training ministers and lay people for the work of the ministry. He has authored 39 books including the fifteen-time best seller, The New Life ... The Start of Something Wonderful (with over 2 million books sold), and more recently, The Miracle Results of Fasting.

The Pacesetter's Path telecast is Dave's weekly television program seen over a syndicated network of secular stations. Dave has produced over 90 audio cassette programs including the nationally acclaimed School of Pacesetting Leadership which is being used as a training program in churches around the United States, and in Bible schools in South Africa and the Philippines. He is a popular speaker at conferences, seminars, and conventions. His speaking ministry has taken him across America, Africa, Europe, Asia, and other parts of the world.

Along with his wife, Mary Jo, Dave established The Dave and Mary Jo Williams Charitable Mission (Strategic Global Mission), a missions ministry for providing scholarships to pioneer pastors and grants to inner-city children's ministries.

Dave's articles and reviews have appeared in national magazines such as Advance, The Pentecostal Evangel, Ministries Today, The Lansing Magazine, The Detroit Free Press, and others. Dave, as a private pilot, flies for fun. He is married, has two children, and lives in Delta Township, Michigan.

You may write to Pastor Dave Williams:
P.O. Box 80825
Lansing, MI 48908-0825

Please include your special prayer requests when you write, or you may call the Mount Hope Global Prayer Center anytime:
1-517-327-PRAY

Published by

DECAPOLIS
PUBLISHING

For a catalog of products, call:

1-517-321-2780 or

1-800-888-7284

or visit us on the web at:

www.mounthopechurch.org

Mount Hope Ministries

Mount Hope Missions & International Outreach
Care Ministries, Deaf Ministries & Support Groups
Access to Christ for the Physically Impaired
Community Outreach Ministries
Mount Hope Youth Ministries
Mount Hope Bible Training Institute
The Hope Store and Decapolis Publishing
The Pacesetter's Path Telecast
The Pastor's Minute Radio Broadcast
Mount Hope Children's Ministry
Sidewalk Sunday School
The Saturday Care Clinic

When you're facing a struggle and need someone to pray with you, please call us at (517) 321-CARE or (517) 327-PRAY. We have pastors on duty 24 hours a day. We know you hurt sometimes and need a pastor, a minister, or a prayer partner. There will be ministers and prayer partners here for you.

If you'd like to write, we'd be honored to pray for you. Our address is:

MOUNT HOPE CHURCH
202 S. CREYTS RD. LANSING, MI 48917
(517) 321-CARE or (517) 321-2780
FAX (517)321-6332 TDD (517) 321-8200

www.mounthopechurch.org
www.gospelmedia.com/
            davewilliams.asp
email: mhc@mounthopechurch.org

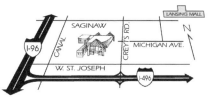

West of the Lansing Mall, on Creyts at Michigan Ave.

For Your Spiritual Growth

Here's the help you need for your spiritual journey. These books will encourage you, and give you guidance as you seek to draw close to Jesus and learn of Him. Prepare yourself for fantastic growth!

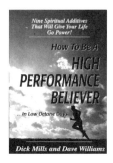

HOW TO BE A HIGH PERFORMANCE BELIEVER
Pour in the nine spiritual additives for real power in your Christian life.

SECRET OF POWER WITH GOD
Tap into the real power with God; the power of prayer. It will change your life!

THE NEW LIFE . . .
You can get off to a great start on your exciting life with Jesus! Prepare for something wonderful.

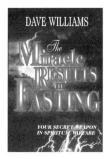

MIRACLE RESULTS OF FASTING
You can receive MIRACLE benefits, spiritually and physically, with this practical Christian discipline.

WHAT TO DO IF YOU MISS THE RAPTURE
If you miss the Rapture, there may still be hope, but you need to follow these clear survival tactics.

THE AIDS PLAGUE
Is there hope? Yes, but only Jesus can bring a total and lasting cure to AIDS.

These and other books available from Dave Williams and:

DECAPOLIS PUBLISHING

For Your Spiritual Growth

Here's the help you need for your spiritual journey. These books will encourage you, and give you guidance as you seek to draw close to Jesus and learn of Him. Prepare yourself for fantastic growth!

THE ART OF PACESETTING LEADERSHIP
You can become a successful leader with this proven leadership development course.

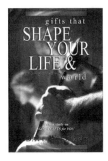

GIFTS THAT SHAPE YOUR LIFE
Learn which ministry best fits you, and discover your God-given personality gifts, as well as the gifts of others.

GROWING UP IN OUR FATHER'S FAMILY
You can have a family relationship with your heavenly father. Learn how God cares for you.

SUPERNATURAL SOULWINNING
How will we reach our family, friends, and neighbors in this short time before Christ's return?

THE GRAND FINALE
What will happen in the days ahead just before Jesus' return? Will you be ready for the grand finale?

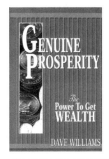

GENUINE PROSPERITY
Learn what it means to be truly prosperous! God gives us the power to get wealth!

These and other books available from Dave Williams and:

DECAPOLIS PUBLISHING

For Your Spiritual Growth

Here's the help you need for your spiritual journey. These books will encourage you, and give you guidance as you seek to draw close to Jesus and learn of Him. Prepare yourself for fantastic growth!

SOMEBODY OUT THERE NEEDS YOU
Along with the gift of salvation comes the great privilege of spreading the gospel of Jesus Christ.

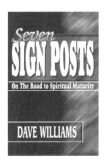

SEVEN SIGNPOSTS TO SPIRITUAL MATURITY
Examine your life to see where you are on the road to spiritual maturity.

THE PASTORS PAY
How much is your pastor worth? Who should set his pay? Discover the scriptural guidelines for paying your pastor.

DECEPTION, DELUSION & DESTRUCTION
Recognize spiritual deception and unmask spiritual blindness.

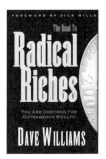

THE ROAD TO RADICAL RICHES
Are you ready to jump from "barely getting by" to Gods plan for putting you on the road to Radical Riches?

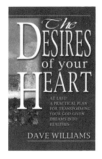

THE DESIRES OF YOUR HEART
Yes, Jesus wants to give you the desires of your heart, and make them realities.

These and other books available from Dave Williams and:

DECAPOLIS PUBLISHING

For Your Successful Life

These video cassettes will give you successful principles to apply to your whole life. Each a different topic, and each a fantastic teaching of how living by God's Word can give you total success!

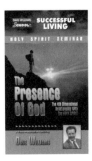

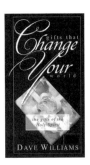

THE PRESENCE OF GOD
Find out how you can have a more dynamic relationship with the Holy Spirit.

FILLED WITH THE HOLY SPIRIT
You can rejoice and share with others in this wonderful experience of God.

GIFTS THAT CHANGE YOUR WORLD
Learn which ministry best fits you, and discover your God-given personality gifts, as well as the gifts of others.

THE SCHOOL OF PACESETTING LEADERSHIP
Leaders are made, not born. You can become a successful leader with this proven leadership development course.

MIRACLE RESULTS OF FASTING
Fasting is your secret weapon in spiritual warfare. Learn how you'll benefit spiritually and physically! Six video messages.

A SPECIAL LADY
If you feel used and abused, this video will show you how you really are in the eyes of Jesus. You are special!

These and other videos available from Dave Williams and:

DECAPOLIS
PUBLISHING

For Your Successful Life

These video cassettes will give you successful principles to apply to your whole life. Each a different topic, and each a fantastic teaching of how living by God's Word can give you total success!

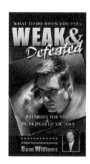

HOW TO BE A HIGH PERFORMANCE BELIEVER
Pour in the nine spiritual additives for real power in your Christian life.

THE UGLY WORMS OF JUDGMENT
Recognizing the decay of judgment in your life is your first step back into God's fullness.

WHAT TO DO WHEN YOU FEEL WEAK AND DEFEATED
Learn about God's plan to bring you out of defeat and into His principles of victory!

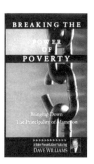

WHY SOME ARE NOT HEALED
Discover the obstacles that hold people back from receiving their miracle and how God can help them receive the very best!

BREAKING THE POWER OF POVERTY
The principality of mammon will try to keep you in poverty. Put God FIRST and watch Him bring you into a wealthy place.

HERBS FOR HEALTH
A look at the concerns and fears of modern medicine. Learn the correct ways to open the doors to your healing.

These and other videos available from Dave Williams and:

DECAPOLIS PUBLISHING